JOHN MARTIN
COLLECTED POEMS VOLUME 9
ALL THIS FUSS

Published by Bysshe-Mendel Verlag

bysshemendelverlag@gmail.com

Copyright © John Martin 2016

John Martin asserts his moral right to be identified as the author of this work

ISBN 978-0-9934630-0-6

Printed and bound by Short Run Press Limited, Exeter

All rights reserved. No part of this publication may be reproduced, stored in a retrieval system, or transmitted, in any form or by any means, electronic, mechanical, photocopying, recording or otherwise, without the prior permission of the publishers.

ALL THIS FUSS

John Martin

Bysshe-Mendel Verlag

Je ne vois qu'infini par toutes les fenêtres

Baudelaire

At last, in this hollow aftermath
amongst the echoes of what was not said
but which I struggle to say to you now,
knowing I cannot get through
to your restless inquietude
(one way of putting it)
with no ultimate assuaging
till you sank down,

                     rooted yet rootless,
there was no growth and you
groaned
          under the weight
of your pain, constant and ruthless
despite all your thrashing of limbs
unable to escape, drawn
by your own gravity to darkness
that has left you safe from your needs.

What would you say to me, then,
if we should meet, that would slow
down all my vivid and desperate
apprehensions of everything lost,
to a calm meeting of minds?

Even dead you must have smarted
under my quibbling tongue:
can you forgive? You might warm me
yet, some comfort in the cold
loneliness where you have slipped
from all possibility of a tender
touch or smile, to sow in your bare field,
amongst the stubble,
                winter's bite
on the hard crust smattered with frost.

Is there some meaning to this
beyond the jumble of words,
some purpose in all this swirling of loss:
I see no saviour
                but the stars look down
in their empty splendour and the dawn
breaks out like a bud of promise -

far from harvest and hard-won fruit,
the dirt crumbles as I pick through,
with dull fingers,
                the withered tilth,
rank with promiscuous weeds
that have forgotten all names,
till I remember the birds,
                how their song
fills time with insatiable sadness
and a slight hope, tremorous as the first stalk,
vulnerable and immortal, on waste ground,
coltsfoot,
              foretaste and memory
of the consuming sun.

Are you talking to me?
                Despite the years
I have lain here, cold and alone,
as you guessed, sleep has not cured me.
Your words through the dark
forage my ear, from a hive splintered
to echoes, voice crackling as an old radio:

that night and for what cause,
you enquire?
              It matters little, how

I came to be here, - but I will recall:
you almost provided a reason
for staying alive;
           I wanted to hurt
and I wanted to heal and gave
what I could - you taught me to laugh:

what shall we call these things?
I was not in love, but liked you,
who lit up my day, and I cared;
about you and how you would be;
but it wasn't enough:
              I knew
I must wound and that wounding
empowered;
           reparation by kindness
as commonplace. Neither of us
stilled the other's desires, but tried,
with scant chance of success,
to put it all right, till,
              as the clock ticked away,
I knew it could never work,
and that's why, that night.

Let us unwind and go back,
to our first time, that encounter
you called a melting, in part, of ice-ghosts.

We both tried hard to make it work,
each in our own way; there were separate
impediments -
           it was not all my fault!
I was imprisoned, I know,
in puritan strictures I finally broke through
and in that freedom found my only protection:

cold logic;
        the body a mechanism, of which
one function pleasure, though it rubbed
their faces in it, those who measured the good.

I hardly need tell you your world
was as barren, and ended up excluding,
as mine, all hope of solutions:
        first, pure soul,
your Shelley phase, and then,
because you had repressed desire's expression,
you concentrated on that as the only way -
Shelley still, as it seems to me.
But then we separated.
        And finally it hurt me
that someone else ignited your hope,
as though you needed to make
me jealous, or so you think.
And that's enough: let me sink
back into this dark hole where at last I am home.
Come, join me, if you wish -
we could barely fondle -
certainly not fuck, - I have no flesh,
but there are sharp bones to remind
how I stuck in your throat.
You gentled me once,
and you were different, in affection,
caressing - why can't you accept
that I needed more than just you,
that rarely two people fill
the full spectrum,
        that all of us
need to find out a home
and to travel at large?

That I held back nothing

from you and gave all I had,
                        all I could?

Who is actually speaking
when I write down the sounds
I am making? What is voice
but an artefact of perpetuated
instances?
            And what am I doing
in this town I will never call home,
looking as I pass through; and no place
my own, either, in that other dreamland
where for some time I pretended to be alive
in a decayed city of broken-down
aspiration and wandering peoples
searching for settlement.
                        I did my best
with the rules to find them security,
more out of defiance than any
conviction that things could change,
this country become a haven
for strangers, conscious
that all these years,
                despite
the referrals, I have no more settled
myself than a migrant seeking
a welcome shore in the face
of indifferent hostility
and the stories warning of aliens.

Shall I pay for my funeral now
or just drink away my days
and somebody else can pick up the bill
at that time;

                    it need hardly concern
me how I am spoken about
when no longer there,
                    but is that
different in some way from what
has been said all along since my parents
worried that I was strange and calmed
themselves with assurances
that in time I would surely
grow out of it.

                    I suppose I have grown,
old, certainly, and out of it was a way
of putting: disconnection,
                    not quite right -
I was never that, but managed a while
to survive, fooling most of the people
most of the time
                    so that what is said
of me bears no relation to anything
when I am finally wanted: dead or alive.

I have nothing that's wholly mine;
and no sense of belonging to one
or the other; not proud at the killing
or pleased to be killed;
                    nations proclaim
a coherence, but I have skirted
this theme with a different view:
to be detached,
                    but to see doomed races
rise and then fall is to feel some sense
of glory, and a spent nostalgia,
though only in passing, and I am not
of them, yet I am with them,

and my throat could catch
at the resonance of all anthems equally;
but I am not for exclusion,
                        margin-people,
shore-wanderers, for I too am lost
in imagining, but look for no country
to keep me safe;
                        always I have walked
away, not wanting to own or be owned,
though I celebrate your purpose,
your unity, but I break off
to an exile only,
                        better to be lost
than to be swallowed, which is my
experience, something I will not change.

You have settled, I expect,
after these many years, into what?
If the light of day lit up this disarray,
if full exposure there of all your decay -
I don't know what survives, bones
and some hair, but where would it stick,
with no flesh?
                        Clearly, you,
as I knew you, are not there,
and I have accumulated my desires
to an accretion of wishing
to have you back, hurt as you did,
but I have stood it, these years of handling
whatever is thrown.
                        I look at your grave
and think: am I unravelling at last,
too much to withstand - would they let me lie,
when finally hunched up into nothing,
in a part of your grave, and would

I be silent then or still enquiring
why it could not work out
to a mutual fulfilment
                          with no loss of vigour.

It is a long seduction going on:
she seems drunk and he, triumphant
in his power of persuasion, conquest
to be proud about;
                          let them talk.
I think of other times, when
you were there, we too compliant
to words, to touch, no difference then?
I do not think I forced you
to be mine, but yet
I hesitate:
                  need is a tyrant
and it bullies us - we both knew that,
and can you blame me when
you sought me out, to stay,
and we each found ways to cheat
the world of its familiar grief,
speaking, it seemed, one language
that both understood, not what they print,
but common speech,
                          the usual words,
passing between us as a key
to opening, but which also locked shut.

It is said we are tempered by loss.
How is this so, for we are not
de-carbonised iron, sharp steel,
but soft creatures with needs
that are seldom quenched.

Time, too, they say, heals
all wounds, but that is also untrue,
we just dig deeper into ourselves
to hide from the pain.
                    Yet the metaphors
which we use to get by, and the dreams
we recall, speak of a deeper swell,
of the breaking of bonds, departures,
a forgotten farewell,
                    some twisting apart
we expect, yet we shy from each time
it appears. Take my familiar story
of ships sailing and I left behind,
or the plane taking me thousands of miles
to a derelict land:
                what does it mean?
The message is clear, though hard
to detect: when you feel the desertion,
alone and abandoned, and know
you are nothing at all, accept to your core
the desolate sense of your loss,
deformed under stress;
                 you are ductile
and tough, can be stretched to perform,
and are perfectly forged.

Ships were always emblems
of my imagination; on them or in
my dreams, as they slide off the slipway
to splash, or sink down,
                slowly, bow first,
waves melting over the hull
with a calm caress; and the deep,
dark rivers that lead from the sea.
My earliest recall the deck, a hot

sun as the fog of this land burnt off
and I looked up to my father
who laughed and threw overboard
wool underwear, once more
free of the frost in those people's eyes
by the sweep of his arm;
                              or, standing alone
as it dipped right under the mouthing
wave, and how do we stay afloat,
yet the rhythm still beats,
part of the ocean throb, the wild salt
of the sea disdaining the baked freshness
from rolls and starched cloths;

once, high above at the rail, the couple
who broke the rules, married against
convention and were cast out, stood
with their children,
                              and then, forgotten the doll,
on the quay below, my father, with all his force,
unfurling his arm to a full sweep, lobbed it up
and over to land on the deck at their feet
and it seemed all separation healed
by that one gesture,
                              faithful and strong,
though the recurrent dream is always
the foundering ship which I do not leave.

Today we fly back; our best apparel
put on. All packed too early and ready
to leave at dawn, passport in hand;
then the slow wait, the airport
conjuring crowds away, threshold
to a new self;
                      some hours yet,

we take lunch on the roof, promised,
last treat of the stay, wearing our caps
in this hot climate.
     Look, I exclaim,
that is our plane, getting ready to fly.
Suddenly and with no warning
my mother cries, her face breaking
in fragments I cannot mend, how
have I hurt her so, as she crumples it
into her hand, and an adjacent stranger, neat
in a silk cheongsam, cries too,
not for her child, but some solidarity
with a mother, to heal all woes;
and they both sob now, - this weeping
of women should be proof against
timetables and schools, even the games
waged by men; but it is not so, and I cry too,
it bursts like a bubble,
       but nothing released;
we board, careless as unconsoled,
and settled down to a flight
through brilliant skies and repetition
of voices from cartoons of the deranged
by their distance from home.

The services I went to as a child
told me about the better way to live.
I took the other path, but kept
the stories of how best
we must love:
     here and beyond.
I never trusted a divinity;
that seemed obsequious, giving up sense,
spilt blood in sacrifice,
fierce rain

to wash us clean - from what?

Thus followed sin with what I learnt
of heaven; there, too, deceived:
learning by heart the pain
of wanting another: abstract, ambiguous
but palpable, for which none of my poets
prepared me
          and to love as I did
was hell, where I have settled.
I never let go,
                    but now you must leave,
no more struggle to trust,
that bleeding of us into
and out of the self; delinquent, and
clandestine, your searching for who
you were; and were
is where you indelibly are,
well past now and way beyond me.

I expected split heavens,
fountains of light and a stretched out
hand to strike, to scour from
flesh the gross enchantments of lost
imagination, the wrinkles
of age;
          but he said
wade through the brackish stream
with patience, calling it hope.

I would not have baulked
at the harsh penances of endurance,
but this, these dull and unmomentous
waters, what can I gain
from such simple, such ordinary task?

Seven times seven, and more,
I have bathed in that muddy river,
and waited again for my skin
to shine as a child's,
                        trusting
the scratched voice
that has echoed through dreams:
the marvellous miracles failed,
therefore why not turn
to the mundane tide of the daily
flow which is all
that we have, to go on or get by.

I will speak no English now, my own
language dead, talk only in others'
tongues, dumb at a stroke.
                        Some
poets I will keep: Shelley, of course,
Jonson, Donne, Hardy and Blake; Yeats;
the Romantics; and all the Victorians;
Brooke, Gurney, MacNeice, Spender;
then those Americans; the three
Thomases; Causley, and Bernard -
wait, why not mention them all
- the list ejusdem generis
to include anyone writing
verses in English, unending
etcetera?
            It was not poets
who mangled the language;
though the more used by liars,
those with something to sell,
poets must move nearer to nonsense,
to un-name nothing when everywhere

slogans signify satisfactions undreamt-of
till we were told what we lacked. No,
English must into the desert
to be unspoken,
                    to shed persuasion,
to know what it feels like to die,
till when we say stone or water
we are no longer fooled
by comparisons of their worth;
is it the fault of poets that marketing
transformed metaphor into a slow puncture
and draining away
                    of meaningful speech?

No longer young, and overweight,
plodding the muddy lane
with the concentration of philosophers,
pounding a path of exercise
to find again some youth,
while keepers of dogs talk familiarly
as to growing children or elders now
in decline and all is sturdy
                    as season's growth,
while the hedges' promiscuous, intemperate
flaunting of crescence augments
our bewilderment, running or strolling -
all go nowhere
                    in this search,
and should stop, to consider
we are only moments
of time,
          nothing eternal,
drop by drop forgetting
what we have been, and coming, then,
maybe, only, out of,

                    and into, our own.

There is no taking away the lonely
endeavour of being alive -
                    our bodies
can cover up for a while;
not that I found a body
other than fraud - yours or mine,
it comes to the same, we are torn
apart by the need to secure,
the urge for more, and break, thereby,
what might have just been enough.
For time, perhaps, but if more
than that, you must let me pass,
for all that I know is only
the passing of time,
                    the tick of the clock.

Time, with the tick of a clock
I hear,
        I feel the pulse as it goes,
the tock of a beat, for time
is a clock that tells only each
passing moment:
                slow the movement
of hands touching the face, and now,
some tenderness, at least, would alleviate
the sense of alone -
                but into a void,
a losing of all time is,
the rhythm, the rhyme,
I will not go.
                For time is loss,
and I stay with time

though it means I have nowhere
but now to go
          where I willingly fall.

We stop at Accrington, and it looks,
from the train, to have the usual outlets
for food, amusements, ubiquitous
chains: *we are not in decline*: the sure
signs of growth, though I hear
the echoes on cobbled streets
of hurrying feet -
          who cares,
that a hundred years have gone
since these men were wiped
from their lives
         and who knows
them now;
         they come back, into
town, and try their keys in the doors
of streets that spread
like the rays of a wheel; and
the doors stay shut:
         such that frozen children
tell us our fate today, effigies
of disconnection, so far
removed from those men of this town
who died, far from what
brought them up
         and seems to have
let them down.

But they will come back,
these men of the north and wipe
the smirk from the faces

of those who scraped in, and then
crowed as at triumph;
                    not to a new
Jerusalem, but to taking away
those few connections we had,
to a paper wedding:
                    we are not
one nation; they lied -
about Scotland, for instance;
these offspring of cash, once cast off,
who rail their frustrated
revenge;
          fostered by time
and experience, no recognising
by parents of children, by children
of parents, so why should they speak
of love, when it seems to them weak,
a sapping of will -
                    they bite hard
not to feel their intolerable pain,
and it comes as a smirk,
                    bland faces
contorted as grimace, they barely
conceal their glee at how far
they have distanced themselves
from affection's exchanges
                    met in the street.

With or without you I will climb
the summit of Loughrigg -
                    I almost wrote *longing* -
to see the lake spread itself
out into distance, glacier-ghost,
the slow thaw of time;
                    but no understanding

between us, now, as then, -
it is all mirrors, the lake too;
but of what reality? How many words
must I speak, or you, before it is read,
before a need meets its assuaging?
But it should be simpler still,
as a creator of all there is
must do yet leaves it to us,
not even that, but without any help,
except for the trees,
      to fill in the void -
as if it needed that we were
the ones
   that would warm up this cold,
with only a bland instruction
       to find
out a way.

How I have over these fells
wandered, to find you, to find
any brightness to dull my need,
to bring me closer
      to letting go;
out of my grasp, though it means
you fall, as I, into a trapeze-twirling
without net, swan-flapping, not flying
now, but making to drown,
or we are tossed on bull-horns,
myth-heavy,
     and sink;
but I tread paths gone over
before by much older feet, and want
to put down
     what I carried -
a burden of debt, and memories'

slow rubbing away of change
until there is only now,
                        and me caught
in between,
                no longer I, but for my name,
calling me back, and I cannot hide.

Into water, to drown, or from height fall;
sink in mud - it is the same extinction
of self I want, into a nothing,
not to merge, no coalescence
of selves,
                others thinking selfishness
into the illusion of being one.

We are separate and divided,
time has taught me that,
as if I didn't sense it was always so
from first nothing.
                        I find the strain of words
and of placing them falters me now

as I seem to be trying to put
inexactness into its proper place,
into a mess, a mixture of moments,
buried alive or dropping deep down,
which way, into a silence,
a not being able to speak -

stuttering, stammering, no words
come to lip, I am stuck,
unable to say how much
I now find myself weak.

My skin smells like another animal -
I can breathe it into my being as a solace
for lost self;
              they walk past,
hand in hand, or, halting, on stick,
on arm of a life-time companion, secure
in affection, no need of a proof.

I peruse them, their faces tell
of the pain, of the joy, of experience,
of trust or betrayal, it is all irrelevant now,
something long past
                  which has shaped them,
not something they would seek to test,
to recall; I still feel separate
from this throng of the satisfied, cut off,
into owning myself
                  less than they are,
each day coming back,
and more, to a time when I fed,
but only through what I now lack.

It could be anyone, having gone
to the bar, eyes meet, and you will see me
through time to a mirroring
of glances that sharpens my wants.

When we are no longer seeking
to use our bodies to make us real,
will I know then that a look
from your eyes will make my eternity last?

Take me out of the now, which is all
I can own, to a splendour, a shining,
a god, or a king, high on his throne.

And shall I touch down?
Or will words spoil and enhance,
as they always do, whereby I am thrown.

Not in awe, in submission, in fear -
think not to be cowed by sky-kingdoms
or bowing-down caliphates, -
that's all these days, we must strive
to fend off if they seek
                              to deny
the falling tunes of what I have
undecided, my sometimes dance,
my inviolate recoil from all
the certainties that make them
kill -
      yet I am drawn
into their ritual of death,
as they cannot live with our
casual breath, the imbalance of love
as a human thing, not what
god-like would make us bend
the knee or bow down:
                        I could just about
stomach a dying god, though
he must not wake up.

Vengeful, they taunt with their certain
stories, seem strong; clamour
a different peace, hush, no questions,
made by the sword into an obedient
quietude, only another way of being
lost, of being found; they have ceded
control, they feel, so sure they are right
as they cross the threshold that leads

to devouring heaven.

                       I too am losing
control of the self, but not as a servant
of power:
              my senses drift,
as streams that snag on a stone
they swirl and are twisted awry,
creased out into fast flowing,
urgent,
              indolent, melting away.

The singular brilliance
of a bright moment -
                    is that all we have,
the rest re-construction into
ways of putting it, explanation,
exculpation, I will not make
the same mistake
next time,
           but always do,
the disappointment boring
and desperate
              leading to a resolve
not to be so open
to hope
        nor think I can
manage the pain
by avoiding the same,
and it works for a time
till I do it again.

Rhyme seems to suggest
it will be all right

in the end:
          the more anxious,
the more I must rhyme,
the more keep time,
you can tell now I am
falling away from the smooth
talking with which I began these lines
into old modes of bewilderment,
words clotting,
          I am tightening up;
this will coagulate to the strict
structures I used once to keep in
unruly emotions, spilt out
but stuffed back,
          till everything fits,
the disconsolate patterning
holding me in -
fragmented and falling to bits.

Broken this way, disintegrating,
mixed-up memories, I could switch
into other languages, a relief
from relentless English, in which
I have mostly said what I feel;
but it pales
          beside Greek;
and German has entered my soul
as a split in the self;
          Yiddish
drawn partly from that, though
more ironic, not so abstruse,
Hebrew the difference, once dead,
like that, but for texts, then brought back,
as Irish or Welsh, Celts
telling us off;

and Romance:
while the north has long nights
where harsh consonants speak to the rock,
south vowels are round, a warm
beach re-echoed, fragrance of fruit;
Russia, its cognates rougher,
and then further east -
hànyǔ floating through
in all its varieties, though stable
in script; but there comes a limit
to how many we learn -
I never really left English.

Mama-loshen, how much I leave
but do not cease to yearn,
this mongrel tongue has survived
so much assault as to be spoken
by almost everyone -
               then what hope
poetry, little understood, that draws
from witches, to summon up,
curse or make lament,
               until
you remember it can also
bring circling aircraft to land.

Iambic pentameter is a fraud,
which I use all the time, well-practised
in its unfolding
               whenever I am about
to deceive. How do we tell
the truth, avoiding devices
that ornament a simple statement:
the more we break down

the more moving away
from saleable utterance; stacked
counters, heaped-up as produce,
fruit and vegetables grown
from the imagination,
                    books
to sell, another commodity
set out:
          how to spend
money and feel well.

If each separation repeats
an earlier one, what was the first cause
of the wound:
               mother-loss,
they all say, which brings awareness
of self, of being alone:
                    no one
without the other.

Then every child is hurt this way,
to spend its life seeking to heal that
primal breach?
               If so,
why does the world not bleed
itself into inconsolable grief,
and rage against all our wrongs?

Paradise barred, we must build
a new world: lonely
responsibility without a god
to guide; far worse an implacable, hidden
face that rules what we do,
which we can't brush aside,

with all we have lived over years,
experiences' slow corrections;
                   or from all that we read
of how humans belong to the earth,
but do so with everything else,
which is not
                   in that rule from above:

something was turned
in the telling -
                   the truth:
the serpent was god.

That was way beyond the possibility
of redemption -
                   to spurn a saviour
brings down opprobrium,
fire and brimstone, it says,
some heavenly anger,
but humans have done it too,
warm flesh flaking as ash.

And will no doubt do it again,
it is not over yet,
                   the rage
of kings and of infants -

is that one howling
into the night a mammalian
perturbation at withdrawn nipples
leading to all this fuss?

Like cast seed I place my words,
not for now-accolades,

                    not my need,
but for one not yet born,
who revives me, wondering
who this was
            fingering out who I am.

I was always lost, does that mean
able to be found, yet, picking over
my bones will not discover more
from that bed than I am

                    and why
bother to speak in a time of lies
when we thirst for a truthful voice,

as some German said.

Walking into a ruined house
whose roof leaks, water streaming
down walls,
            how do we get this fixed.
to live with some comfort.

I worked in this once and my dreams,
for this was just that, must spring
from those days, but also
from something else -
the house I was in was not habitable;

that is still my dream: tearful voices
on all sides;
            perhaps I have had enough
of this disrepair - let it all fall down,
with nowhere to be at home.

In this world godhead is not
to be found,
    Shekhinah-exile
from first expulsion
to homelessness, exile, a long trek
 - away from - towards - what -
some promised land?

Maybe tomorrow, - meanwhile
rest here a space, not to settle,
sink roots, leaf and be fruitful,
for this is all desert,
     but along the way
there was harvest with some love
for the shining faces of those
who had worked in the fields, at the looms,
in the mills, down the mines;
     sure, they were paid
wages, that left others able
to calculate profit - so they all gained
by exchange and acknowledged
some god, as ever,

though most of it hidden, as now,
perhaps he just clouds his face.

Exiles: have fled countries at war,
dead economies, absolute doctrines,
drown or land, some, on
a European shore,
    and threaten, thence,
tunnels and other ways of travelling
to an England that seems haven -

though all clogged up with European

confusion: we came to your habitation,
re-shaped it to our purpose,
looked up and down you,
finally forced to leave, the Queen
smiling benign
                    over bloated state-heads
stuffing their pockets with cash
that usually flows from power;

and who to blame -
those who dilute the fact
of conquest, rape, enslavement:
each of us, lonely
or nation, repeat
from this our myth
of triumphant
                    salvation,
dunkirking out of defeat.

History, reconstruction
of lost memory,
                    is not to be trusted;
but all nows follow
its curve through time, whereby
we can see ourselves
in a mirror of what is past:
as disembodied, disembedded paradigms
of a sometime paradise when
we tended, spun, milked, sowed, tilled,
and picked, gathering up, at seasonal
norms, at one with growth
and demise;
                    when the first fall,
and from what?

But we landed on our feet, and then
came chronicles, all false,
made up or touched up,
where our superb capacity for deceit
left you to guess what we went through,
remembered, imagined,
and this was the truth, more or less.

No less true what imagination
holds than it happened that way:
who knows, who cares -
we are all stories waiting to be read
off our tombs, though they are usually short,
dates - of birth and of death;
and, sometimes,
    much loved;

stone masons can do no more
than carve such words,
for them price only,
but the bereaved think
it makes some difference
to have strict stone, letters
that speak of connection, remorse,
some bond with the dead;

small comfort to me,
that slight slab, covered
with old leaves I cleared
with my foot:
    it says nothing at all,
nothing: unless we were that.

I have cried, put my mind
to every abstraction, every

alchemical raising up of inert
dirt from the dullness of death:
how many words I expend
you are not to be found.

This knowledge of loss is personal
and abstract;
              I know nothing
about tribes, or wandering peoples
other than what I read; of what it means
I can work out something;
                      I knew those
who spoke of bereavement
as permanent grief; others were not so sure,
maybe as mixed-up as me,
                 though they covered it
better than I do with all that experience,
superior to the theories I gleaned from texts.

All dead, and others since then;
me next, I suppose;
              at times
I can only welcome
a simple silence, voiceless, -
yet they still sing, for strong
and loud in my ears, perpetual
and momentary, sounds
and dissolves their song.

Our only possibility of survival
as sane humans:
             disobey
divine commandments;

our imagination, it is true,
has inherited all the cultures
of killing and exclusion,
as well as the formation
from need and desire
                    of gods
to direct and punish
all deviation:
                take your pick,
and fight to the death
to establish the truth:
                    until
we accept that the crying child
who is not of our tribe
must have all of our love,

we have not understood,
not even begun to imagine
how far we have strayed.

Let me be mongrel, atheist
and an exile: nowhere belonging
and to no-one subject: my blood, I expect,
could be sucked up in syringes
and tested for various signifiers
of purity -
                but I know none will be found:

I came out of the sea, the forest,
from the high mountain and farmed
the valleys - seeds in my gut tell this -

a poor species that never had
the superb regnance of great predators,
but teamed up to hunt

and transferred it to kings, tyrants,
priests, demagogues and slick
spreaders of slogans:
                            even if they smirk
bland, they are on the prowl,
and always ready to kill,
with a knife, with a gun,
with a bomb,
                with a smile, with a poem.

Track my ancestors in my veins,
blood-sucker-doctors
                            with steel proboscis -
what will you find - that
I am descended from abstractions
of statistics, muted into curves
of chronology -
                fuck that.
Who I am does not depend
on what was, or who were they -
I am now, separate, searching my way.

We share similar genealogies,
seeking the same tombstones,
that tell us nothing about what we are
and how we are meant to behave.

This picking through blood
to find forebears forgets
how many great-, great-, great-,

great-, great-, and so on, there isn't space
on the page to expand -
                so many
great-great-grand-parents common to all.

The days blurred and she forgot
what she had become and lived
once more as a child
                    in Accrington market,
the town still sore at that time,
though none dared say how deep
the wound from the war;
                    haunted,
but ghosts don't feel the soft warmth
of black pudding nor sink their teeth in
and let it over their lips run
                    spilling
to fall off their chin, comforting as it melted
in her mouth, that moment revived,

in the market, happy at the bleeding into her
of the rich easing of hunger,
                    she forgot
the losses, grief, disappointments
folded away, hurts became temporary
as the rain such that
                    she was in Accrington
market again, in the faltering first steps
of our century, now in the last
crippled forwardness
of inexorable extinction but minded not
when the taste, but most the smell
came back with full force as she would call up
blood sausage,
                    sensuous,
and persistent just at that point
where sense failed, and then, time,
as she smiled into herself
that recurrent instance
                    of Accrington black pudding.

Lancashire towns? I would say,
and we set off from Keighley -
to Colne, Nelson, Burnley
and then Acrington,

                      a ghost town,
no rich throb, deserted
and where were we going?

Almost a hundred years
since the town took the blows
from which even today it has hardly
recovered;

                    they have papered over
the cracks with slogans, nothing
peculiar to this town, bland
as concrete,

            but we two,
bewildered by time, and our pulling
apart, not from each other,
for never together:

                    it was our slight
recognition of how to give
that fed us, kept us alive,
so we drive regularly
through old Lancashire towns
and felt dead as the old inhabitants,
mourning their memories.

Proclaimed at this point
the highest motorway - what worth
that description - it is a bare
landscape, Falklands, we called it once,
by which was meant bleak
and certainly nothing to kill for.

From Rochdale and then Milnrow,
signposted, climb to Saddleworth Moor,
unexplained, sad place of lost childhood;
and then undulate for a while
till Halifax, Huddersfield, lead past Brighouse
to Bradford, my old home where ghosts
proliferate out of broken stone:
                                    I have always been
for exploited people,
                                    do not belong
to the endless, repeated refrain,
by onion-skin men, slogans
slipping off, their song
of austerity for all but themselves -
they are paste, pale-faces, paltry
by comparison with those who strove,
died, both sides of the Pennines,
in towns that sent their men willingly
to a banker's slaughter,
                                    realer than
all these faint faces of phrase -
factors stroking their wealth.

A new voice for this once-striving
party
        that fell into blurb -
and what he says is different
from the simpering sneer
of the neat men, their faces
as clean in deceit as bare arses -

I can't tell the difference;
former leaders, experts at cheat,
exhort further fraud,
and little voices expostulate

their incontinent abstinence,
as if we somehow cared
that they use calculators
to add up their sums.
Win an election and spoil
the people. That's one story.

But beat true as the heart
of our real history, not their
cut-out-from-cardboard heroes
made into fantasy films.
                              Well, maybe
defeat: but rather with you
than their hollow, cockerel
victory to line their own pockets,
smiling all the way to a depleted
indifference: telling the truth,
like poetry, makes no difference,
unless it can sell,
                    but this is not to be bought.

*I distrust your easy use
of the forms I bequeathed,
how you messed about
with my callow lines,
frustrations of flesh,
                    that word
you view with disdain,
a struggle that led to defeat,
which you celebrate,
                    somewhat
relentlessly - perhaps
you could give it a rest.*

I learnt, became capable,

leaving behind that wounded
self,
     not that I healed, but made do,
old griefs a fuel for the fight.

You have not scrupled
to meddle, - you show me to others,
as earnest and febrile;
               I shun what you make
of me, to prove I still flow in your veins
when you have long since dried,
bedding comfortably into my pains.

That stung! How do I riposte?
I always deferred to you and your
statements in hewn stone
of how much you were harrowed:
but where do we meet?
               Which of us bleeds?
How do twin waters that flow
alternately out of, and into, each other,
know where the one begins,
and its shadow, its mirror
cedes
     and then the reverse?

You were meant to be loyal,
that's what you constantly boast,
that you stayed true
when others betrayed.

So why unfaithful to me?
I need you. Have nothing else,
and though we have wandered
through different times,

surely we have a singular voice?

That voice is a fraud:
$$\text{ventriloquist}$$
or doll: which is speaking?
But you wilfully miss my point:

I have survived as interpretable
text, poor carvings on cave-stone walls,
though the dream was hunting.

By what right do you interfere
and re-arrange meanings
that met exactly my state,
even if not to your taste, clumsy
and badly expressed?
$$\text{The politics}$$
of our time, it seems to me,
who, because you reign, and I lost
my voice,
$$\text{is that earlier errors}$$
must be put right by a bland
smoothing away of hope,
and all I then cared about
could be guided into correct thinking,
by twisting the way I feel.

Anyway, it hurts more now, when
the outcomes are fixed and I know
there were other ways forward
you did not take,
$$\text{which seem so clear;}$$

you thought he was able to change
you, to an alternative way
of loving;
   and this would be done
simply by talking; telling your dreams
to reveal new layers of self
as you cast off skin.
    He practised
some sort of magic, alchemy
to transform; but the point was missed:
recalcitrant, stubborn,
    I became
what I was born or what I was made -
who says, and what difference
     does it make?

You know that it didn't work, of course:
he helped: to do your job
amongst strutting men;
    broadened
your outlook, more of a university
than your own, the way you'd approached it,
and above all he brought you back
to a self
   that had sunk so low
in your abject love; though only
when finally abandoned
that attempt to found whole universes
on a single care did you manage to drop
the pain,
   and, for a time, breathe,
in the atmosphere of communicable
folk. And that didn't last. So, free
of that need, you became a resource
for others and played yourself out

to a different tune.
　　　　　　　　　　Drink kept
you sober - and how you drank,
what hidden, hiding your unhealable hurts -

and, so, who is the fraud?

Both of us, then? What do you want,
from me, old man -
　　　　　　　　　don't think
I didn't relate to those
for whom most of their lives was past.

The old particularly engaged
my sympathy and attendance
and I picked up fragments
of wisdom from those exhausted
by their long lives:
　　　　　　　　so tell me -
what is the reason
you are still pulling apart
to find you are held? I wish
you would die and I would be free
to owe you nothing;
　　　　　　　　I did not think
you would gloat over how I went wrong, -
I did not expect to be old, and you,
you don't like it, do you?
　　　　　　　　　Age's
infirmities, lack of attraction, -
you would not have minded a kiss.
I was much harder on this point,
and did not allow touching
　　　　　　　　　without love.
I could have been wrong. And it's too late

for me, but, possibly, not for you.

Touching? To stroke my thighs?
Well, yes, the theory is fine,
but nobody comes by,
                    with willing eyes,
though I sense ambiguities
all the time,-
              yet they do sometimes
smile and I wonder if someone
will warm me before I die
and think it unlikely.

But different for you, and here
we fall out:
              you abstained for so long
and then your desire, fully fixed
only on one, was starved, when you could
have feasted,
              while I, because of my age,
must fast, a hunger-artist, with only the ghost
of that veteran love to warm up my bed.

Then better, perhaps, that we do not meet
to discuss what makes us the same.

Pools in the mud, the tide far out;
pick these stems, they are as bare
as bodies once were
                    or so I imagine;
the horizon a void till a man rides
a horse on the sands, lost from sight.
We wonder how far he has gone,
and, then, another, a second horse, trots,

till they both gallop, far dots
in the distance, -
                    but we, back to picking
the samphire plants, water-logged,

separate, edible, some metaphor
for love, perhaps, until, with vengeance
it rained
          and we drove back
talking about companionship,
not sexual love, thinking that a spasm
for young men, -
                    and such a waste, I felt,
that faltering frenzy to find fruit,

not caring where it should fall.

Across the room someone is laughing:
are we the only species
                    that laughs?
Hyenas don't: it's their cry,
and cry, in the sense of tears,
again, it is only us.
                    Add
languages, and you see why
we rule the world and invent
gods, when ordinary animals
are content simply to be them,
though nearer to humans the more
they attempt to deceive.

Not laughing now: serious
as a storm cloud, nodding
in conversation, sullen and thoughtful -
and my desire fades,

                    but then
a faint smile, and the face lifts -
as a spreading sunrise it clears -
there is a cascading of laughter
that bursts out and I want to go over
and hug, as this
                    a balm for all hurts.

Betrayal a broken promise,
not straightforward,
but double:
                    treason, I understand, -
it works against trust, sells
secrets or from principle
gives them away.
                    Traitors change sides,
break belonging, are not true -
to something that is not felt
to be worth steadfast
adherence:
                    so they shift
allegiance, presumably without
too much struggle of conscience.

In a relationship
                    betrayal is -
stop! I cannot rationalise
such a thing and will say no more.

We trod a land that was like my life,
my love -
                    melodramatic
and impossible: in concrete terms,
channels impeded our stroll,

there was no clear path, and no way
through to the shingle cliffs
                         of the shining shore.

So we turned back and talked
of my dreams.
                    Yours, you keep close,
I do not know how you steer
the deeps, heavy with rocks,
and keep afloat -
                    you do not say.
I am always wary you want to pry
and shut up when you try
to find me out.

Marsh grass, soft in places
and no way through:
                         I was tempted into talking
about that daughter in endless mourning,
whom I chose as emblem;
                              no way out there,
either, so we balanced stones
on a rock, random and precarious,
who knows what the time and tide
will sweep off:
                    those symbols
of all we loved. Nothing
to make them sure, and mine
will surely fall down;
                         you seem
more secure in heaping up stones,
than me; but we left behind
monuments to something lost, safe
in their instability, waiting to drop,

as the sea heaved and relented,
and we were amazed how soon
it went out
        or would,
in recompense, slyly, and swift, come in.

He bumped into the furniture;
Mother scowled,
        averse to drunkards.
How Dad calmed him I do not know,
some soothing, though all he wanted
was money.
        Curious, but ignorant,
I watched with glee this altercation:
she did not trust him, nor
did Dad, but didn't give up.

Another drunkard - why did Dad take me -
his friend and colleague, insulting Dad,
insulting me, as his wife wept, wiping her eyes,
said sorry to Dad,
        he does not mean what he says.

Mother, later, as tears filled her eyes,
told me that when he sang out
it was Mario Lanza, a fine tenor voice,
he could have been famous,
singing *The Student Prince*;
        but mad catches
he bellowed mellifluous, Farfrae airs,
the Scots wandering far from home.
I picked up they were pissed,
        though knew nothing
of how that makes everything bearable,
till I could do it myself,

                   too late
to be one with them, yet remember it still.

Music; loud; it stirs up -
where are you?
                   You would have been
ready for anything in this noise,
and went with it, often,
into a satisfaction
of sorts -
          but it didn't help you
to live, or, maybe it did, after all,
who knows!

Fumbling to bring you back,
(no, that can't be) to a better
understanding of what is past;
I can't work out why you obsess me so,
still, hearkening to a deplete voice.

Poison I sucked gratefully,
and you said as much,
as it spread through my veins.

We could choose someone
                         who seems
the most principled of all; yet
that would make the party unelectable
I read; we are an odd people,
to be swayed by headlines, paper
stories from paper people;
                         perhaps
it is true, that we have no minds
of our own and must be told

how to think, how to vote,
by the minions of rich owners
strutting their desolate halls,
to bring people to right thinking,
stirring up trouble -
                    why? Were they
soon jilted or otherwise failed in love?

This one could make changes,
in alliance with others who find insult
in the brass-necked, baby-faced
purveyors of petty, of paltry
platitudes:
                    these milk-sop liars
with their contempt for the Scots
and for those less fortunate
than themselves:
                    sad boys, alone
and abandoned early in schools,
fighting their way to the top
to make up for so early a betrayal, -
hurt by the wounding
                    could make some kind,
not these, though, surely not to be trusted.

Along the canal-bank -
                    two couples,
and me - not five friends, exactly,
but some of us are, sometimes -
we have known each other,
and worked together, for years,
and, then, partners -
                    we swap
interlocutors as we walk, and talk

of each other, almost gossip,
but also parental in care:
income and alcohol consumption,
concerns at drinking too much-

and this we is exposed
as a fiction, apart from this afternoon
canal-perambulation
                    which seemed
to be apt in the known instances
of a long connection,
                    temperate
and extreme in the glimpses
it gives that those we know
are other
          and endlich always the same.

Forgive if I slip into German
at times, cognate with English,
a pulse still beating, heard in the roots
of words.
          Like the world's waters
poetry partly cleanses pollution from
debased language;
                    this takes time
and its composition is affected
by slow enfolding of the contaminant
into a corrosive bitterness,
                    such that
some things must die to let new life
breathe after that devastation.
Hölderlin answered his own question
in fractured verse, though
it drove him mad.
                    Ireland

is not the same, its statues tell England
to keep its hands to itself;
one language but other, -
they look to writers to make
the difference through honesty
and pain.
        For Hebrew, sacred
and vernacular, I cannot say,
I am not that familiar,
                but I am sure
it will not be able to hide the strain
of its birth and its hard growing.

Above all poetry must make the people,
not slogans;
        loss, maybe, but not profit,
constantly question belonging,
querulous and angry
like Brecht
        and stick to our guns.

I kissed with closed eyes,
as the wise poet wrote,
and dreamt they would open
to find you wrinkled;

weathered, as we aged,
out of all slogans
to a caring that had learnt
to forgive:
        at last I looked,
saw you rise up, fresh
as at that first kiss,
        forever fixed
that time past,

                    and still further away,
smiling, duplicitous,
without substance, a shadow cast,

fleeting as caught breath,
and woke to the same hunger,
the same rage
                    with nothing settled,
nothing assuaged.

Rearranging the past as I play
it out yet again:
                    does that make
me better?
          To think it through once more -
a different conclusion, such as:

I would have fled at once and far away
from you then had I known
                    how it all turned out.

So many times in the history
of what we were I could leave;
to do so now seems a cheat, this mixing up
tenses;
          it doesn't work, that time
or this, - we are lost in a maze
                    where I cannot get out.

The frenzy increases. I drink more.
We are going round in circles
to nowhere -
                    whirligig
that turns time backwards

and forwards, inside and out
and all shaken
to come right in the end.

But it doesn't fall out like that;
new affinities for us to choose,
to place where most fit -
no jigsaw this,

but a jagged fracture of what
I meant, you meant, what,

but leave me alone,
nothing
can ever mean anymore.

Freedom: but not so simple
the pleasures of sex -
yet we are all animals,
embellish it which way you will,
with prayer or poetry,
sonnet-symmetry,
or such-like sonority - it comes
to the same thing:
that we are
reproduction engines, no more than
blown dandelions, octopus-enchantment,
mantis that lost its head, the wild rut:
how they go on,
and on,
led by the nose, driven
mad for so little reward, it seems.
Being human, we call this
desire, quotidian and fatal,
momentary and lasting -

                        it breaks
apart and makes into one
the incredulous heirs
                        of copulation,
sunning their wings, or soon enough,
licking their wounds.

Refuge in alcohol and clichés:
neither authentic being, but what
the hell -
        I am sinking
down, into that state, drinking
my life away, as they say,
trying to sort out truth from the lies -
rhymes stabilise:
I will dispense with stability
and stumble, tumble, fall
into a deep pit of old longing
where I can rot,
                        after all, why not?

I see you are still rhyming?
                        It's an old
habit I must drop, like all the other
accretions of care -
                        let me strip;
stop this pretence that I wear
all that I was as a woven cloth -

and just stand bare.

Until I escape the repeated pattern -
poems or an old attachment,
I won't be free of the urge to rhyme

in metre;
I do my best but am led,
follow a set path:
now I must softly tread
and plant my probing feet in a field,
not mine, but mined, and at all costs
avoid the underfoot bulb of a springtime,
that explodes in my mind,
scurrilous
scent, crude colour, till it burst in my face
and I spit out at last:
no more rhyme.
I must tell the truth. But rhyme's
the least of it - an excuse,
to avoid fumbling for words in the rush
to expression:
so many images
flood our perception, we are drowned
in the surge, floundering
in these promiscuous undulations
of all we desire,
waves of feeling
that come from booze, loud music,
familiar tunes that take us back.

I want to shed that sense,
to wash
it clean, but also free of the need
to strive:
evolution's clamping
of what we learnt. But I do not wish
to survive - you see how there are
rhymes enough to choose
in these lines
but I did not rise

and I will not bite.
    Does that mean I have entered
a purity of utterance, without rhyme,
metaphor, or the balancing of words
in pattern?
            *Not poetry, then, you
are trying to write?* No - I am trying
to find and to tell the truth.

Without artifice? Yes, especially
that sort of thing;
                for this is a personal
record of how I felt, a particular time,
but you keep intruding with tricks
of rhetoric,
            picking up rhymes
as though you needed a shag.

*So, it's come to that,
                once more, -
to sex, or rhyme, which you say
you want to abjure.*

Shakespeare couldn't do Jonson, nor he,
him - they were just different:
                        didn't fall out,
kept friendship alive, drank together
at times,
        till Shakespeare
went back to Stratford and died:
he could hardly drink after that -
but he would have tried.

Ben's epitaph for his mate
was full of wordful relief, and a dig

at his lack of learning
                    which big Ben had,
who also felt he should have blotted out
loads of his lines;
                    tart compliment, then,
to say he burbled, a stream, kept going,
original, inventive, for we know,
young or drunk,
                    very seldom we hit
the mark with our eyes closed - rare-

and most of the time we have
to work at it hard;
                    emblems,
these two of our bewitchment,
                            mystery,
calling, trade.

You assume so many shapes,
all false, feigned, fake - if
I could just for once find you
by force of alliteration, hold you
tight an instant in weakening arms,
not let go;

            was it my fault
you fell? Did I not say I would keep
you firm in my grasp?
                    I fought, faltered,
became feeble; what am I saying -
that I could not form alone what would flame
enough to warm you, keep you alive,
perhaps
            at the cost of my life?

It was only you made the final choice,
in due course;
                       and so I must leave.
And we both know the rest.

But when it comes to betrayal,
memory is the first offender -
some chemical substance laid down
to make this hall of distorting
mirrors-
           remembering is always
a false image, as in a bad reflection;

for that reason alone we should not fear
death, which we feel a wiping clean
of all recollection;
                        for we have already
died, we are not re-living past times
when we recall an instance,
but watching a film
                        where we play
some sort of ourselves
                          into particular
dissatisfaction. What actually happened then
was not part of this
                        reflecting ourselves
in a made-up past.

To be dead is to have no memory,
if memory is what fizzles away
in brains,
           chemical at source
or electrical - what do I know,
or anyone else -

something that troubles
our brains, so long as blood pours
into them, a feeding virtue.
That makes them bold -
             whether
imagining or reminding,
this, for me, is more real
than limbs, than bodies in heat,
shaking away -
          and how could we
live with passion
          if it meant
nothing at all
        and all of us out,
like a light.

They grow as our fingernails, tectonic
plates;
      I have watched mine
lengthen till they break at contact,
tearing, to cause pain;
         but if
they should elongate,
extend down the street to a far
landmark building,
          would it be like the way
collided lands rise into hills
and the slow movement of continents,
endless and immemorial, as we spin round
in such pointless whirligig -
          why think
that any of this could be other
than some mad joke
        or the obscure lines
of a poem that defy translation.

I still practise you, out
of my desolate hands:
                        you live
by this in the plunder of self
and are invaded, made other
than what you wanted to be
out of these incorporate limbs
that stretched your nerves
till you thought they would break.

With me
            you reluctantly stroked
as though we could make wholeness
out of these parts of ourselves,
you, seeking out ways
                        to be free
of what held you back; and I,
to mirror your need,
                        though
we could not see:
                    not the glass
darkly standing between,
                            but the clear

reflection of all we had been,
nor, finally, hide from our selves.

Hard going, uphill, and over,
to punish, prevent
some awkward spilling out
of a lost sense
                of belonging,
calves hard as cast iron;
they will not bend,
those tough-muscled men

who are panting away
their pain,
       on a desolate fell-side,
sheep-tending, without tenderness
to make a new breed,
                calves supple
as soft butter. Simply sensations'
brutality from which blossom
and are born the perishable
fruits of today, which by night
are decayed;
          predators
                roaming the hills
in stately stealth.

I have changed at last, moth-wings
out of caterpillar, cocoon-dreaming
what impossibilities of a present
to where all is actually
            now.

Faithful, writer of sad and angry
sonnets, to a scavenge
of all waste, raptor,
           as Goethe,
hovering over his songs.

Connect to a full communion, swift
withdrawal, the function of wings,
just click, all in an instant:
              at the next
table a woman chatters in German,
unusual accent I cannot place,
though I follow the drift
of sense:

                  she makes herself laugh -
how could I lean over
and ask her
                  woher sie kommt.

So long searching the snow for
Fata Morgana, or sand
                  for a false oasis -
it was always just desert, the same,
waves, dunes or ice,
                  no comfort,
mile after mile, nothing to guide,
but whisperings in the air, cloud-faces,
shadows over the sea.

                  Nowhere
to settle, but keep going, no goal
either just keep moving on, keep
walking , keep repeating
                  solvitur ambulando,
which I misunderstood then
as walking saves you, yet perhaps
the same thing, solving and saving;

I learnt the old texts, drew
theoretical understanding that
it is not the mirage that's fake
and uncapturable,
                  but longing
thrown from the mind, yet
I still went on looking
as they mocked whilst fading away.

Exhibition-aircraft circle the sky

and all crane to see the way
they drop and recover:
                        it's sky-writing,
freehand, escape from the rules,
this spectacular showing off,
taking over the clouds
                        to tumble
and somersault, such aerobatic
performance - could almost be
sex, then, inhibitions melting away.

Till, one day, there is failure -
of judgment? Mechanics?
                        Weather,
perhaps? We don't know yet,
but wonder at which point you must
stop diving
               and start to climb
out of inevitable fall where
you will hit the ground with a certain
aplomb:
              headlines, innocent dead.

Better, surely, to pull out
of a daft manoeuvre
and just climb
              out of sight?

Born soon after the war
(oh, was there only one?)
I grew up believing Germans
were a disease,
            - germ, causing infection,
or the way forward, εαν μη ο κοκκος
του σιτου πεσων

εις την γην αποθανη,
our schoolboy drawings Spitfire
and Messerschmitt dogfights;
comics where stupid Jerries with long legs,
in circumcised helmets, ejaculated
Donner und Blitzen, Schweinhund;
or films in which loudspeakers warned
like gods' messenger: Achtung,
Achtung;
       comb on the upper lip
our understanding of history.

To make fun of it seems like
mocking the dead, that deliberate extinction
of people we do not wish
to believe is human und wenn
ich schreibe Gedichte bin ich
         auch barbarisch?

    .

On fire that time, and still on fire, parts
of the world: little if nothing was done
till too late to save;
       since then we have walked
through the ashes of hope to meet ghosts
haunting the ruins of their lives.

There is still idolatry, masking itself
as a pureness of god, yet they are all
too human.
     But I began with Germans,
almost as bad as it gets, yet have found out
so many subtleties
       surround them
my head swims with the Frage:
why are people still killing Menschen?

Is it because there isn't enough
land - to live on, grow food -
that all the prurient observers
of other species for our titillation
look with intent seriousness,
voyeurs,
        on territories and primacy
being challenged and held onto or lost:
fuck, find food
        (maybe the other way round);
never mind cctv in our city centres,
what about all this Olympian spying
on other creatures in their delight
and their struggle to live.
        Why should we worry
about mere animals, though, when we
are constantly filmed as strange beings
with odd habits and hard cravings?

Often spoken by actors, commentaries
trite as Jack and Jill *and finally he has
his way*, and eaten
        for all his pains.
Perhaps they do really care
about all the planet's inhabitants,
but they are wrong way round
and back to front:

        first find
enough food for all,
        and the rest
would naturally follow. They tell us
how long it has taken for fins to evolve,
providing proper programme-length
entertainment,

                    and they worry
about over-warming
                    and win awards.

You are no ghost, you
are very palpable body, responding
to touch, now, not then; and bring
me alive:
                    awake at last, making
you moan. Crude, brutal even,
seem to be no way tender...
                    except that...
what?...that I author such a response
is what troubles my rest - is it that?
 - and once again I am losing
all sense of control as I spiral
down:
                    is this my last
giving away, to make you pleased -

and now, with you only a dream,
I don't know where or what,
my hand revives you as I feel there
your smell, lingering still,
and I cry
                    but am not consoled.

You, I still emphasise,
                    for you are not
the former bled-dry ghost of my dreams
I have put back in the grave
from its daily rising to haunt,
yes, **you**, begin the new torment's
gradual unfolding.

              Will this lead
to long thirst as I grow ever more
dry in wanting you warm in my arms -
both of us sure, well, nothing lasts,
but your panting subsides
                        and you smile:
I am all at sea not safe
on firm land
              looking at **you**.

So the global corporates embrace
chemistry,
              money-making
that will drug, soothe, excite, awake
us out of a torpor of rhetoric,
wringing us dry-
                  we will take
their tablets, be less worried
at what is going on in the world,
the middle sea spewing up
corpses, and
              why should children ever
arouse more pity than parents evoke,
for all dead bodies are possibilities
lost,
      children, perhaps, more
than most because not yet corrupted
by other than simple needs:
                        we are lost
in their crying and smiles, it is evolution
that beckons, Calvinist, Jansenist,
                        Darwin
completing the full diagram
into a poetry of forms, of colour, of shapes.

That sea, mother of our poetry,
all but trapped between strange
continents, countries changing
their names
                as it stroked up the thighs,
Adriatic, Tyrrhenian, Aegean,
not kissing or cuddling, but proud
in its slaughter,
                        fruits of the dead
ripening on its wide shores.
Not monogamous, this species,
unlike swans;
                we were made
promiscuously, even from gods;
marriage to make us social
but it was kinship that drove blood-feuds.
I don't understand Helen - swan-god-fathered,
yet all too human
                        how she fell for Paris
and all the inexorable murders
following on.
                What should Paris
have done with that flung fruit,
the golden apple, cold and inedible,
strife's backward blessing;
                for how could anyone choose
between victory in war, exorbitant sex
and mastery over the people - though
politicians will have it all.
                        He chose sex
and Troy eventually felt a spread power
wipe out what stood in its way,
religious rites notwithstanding,
burnt to a core, the rest slaves,
tremendous abjection, that night,
when the walls finally fell:

a complete vengeance, the dreadful
slaughter, the tumult and yell
of final revenge:
    the defeat of sex,
its power paltry and pitiable,
now forgotten
    though I remember it well.

Within the year let me be dead
and all affections lost
for the enjoyable things
     all say make
and keep us alive;

not so me, I am down and out,
into the drains of love, as always,
known disappointment, alone,

I tread as ever desolate paths
to nowhere and back,
     circular walk,
hedge woundwort now all but frayed,
into old age -
    I would have said, like me, yet
hedge-bank thickens, all crowd
to seed as the season wanes:

but I do not wish anymore
to be part of this foison,
will let go into seedless
and infinite nonsense,
     no traces
of self, where
    I was at
and what wanted.

Wandering, love's ambassador, through
empty embassies
                    mouthing the right phrases,
compassion, caring, to mask
disappointment at two
                    not disappearing
into one, all theory, *you, my arms, holding*, -
letting go is clearer than
interlocking-for-a-moment-limbs'-explosion:

oh, oh, oh, - fuck that,
                    I am so lost,
and would drown in the welter of hands'
fondling:
            diplomatic solution
out of extremes - just to caress a limb
is to stop
            anger and hatred:
                            yes,
if it stays that way - not my post -
I must secure positions firm enough
to leave room for movement -

not give, with my willing tongue,
pleasure in satisfaction
                    but speech,
balanced and meaningless,
competing slogans to make you buy.

Headlong into destruction, - how, how?
not falling, the inexorable,
                    slow
decline, that unpossession
I always strove for, as you could learn
to relax by tightening your grip -

69

no, this time it is willed and driven
hard into with full negligence
and disregard for all that could sensibly
hold back as though this the last
dice-throw
        and I don't care
which way I spreadeagle and spiral
into the sublime ecstasy
of coming at last into all the vast
and infinite nothing
               of what I was
and no longer am;
           being: a matter
of loneliness and hunger,
but no longer for me.

How shall I tell myself
to the counsellor, who will put me
straight and show the way out
from the way out;
         what stories
pick through together again,
there is nothing new to relate -

that I am mad, certainly,
but no departure there, though my head
now spins faster than ever.
             I was always
out of control but somehow turned
it to dance, lame and broken,
but still steps following time.

That changed. Ready to give up
every pretence that I am sane
and drag myself down till at last

I no longer breathe -
                    everything lost,
so lost, that at last I am found
as singular driftwood
                    on desolate beach.

When god decrees how we should
fuck, how stroke, caress, find
bewildering satisfaction in bodies,
we must stop to consider
                    this deity
telling us that sex must be channelled,
kept within bounds, not allowed
to overflow, and if so,
                    punished -

yes, it is a dangerous impulse,
that ruins lives - see mine, such as
it was -
        but we have to resist,
and we shall not win,
                    but go down
fighting a god that says: punish;

and pleasuring the god that says: love
as much as you can, always
and everywhere:
                    never the need
 to resurrect, always erect,
                    penetrating
right into the cold heart -

                    of the darkening sun.

Erotomania - means I want lots
of sex, and bugger the consequences;

that is, I am not far off dying,
the last surge of the tree, the bush,
this urge to fuck till I drop -
no matter whom,
                    but I need to flower
and then fruit - the deep instinct
that says, for I must soon go,

something has got to survive
this bland sleep,
                    the hard fuck
that takes us over the edge of death
back to a paradise
                    from which
we are not shut out.

Touching your skin, feel
we are one,
                    though it is not so,
for there are frauds running
through all this simulacrum
                    of desire,
pretences that go way beyond
the fictions of literate beings-

we are faking all this, and at which
point I could say it was true,
that some meeting of other than skin

took place
            who knows,

we do not let go, how much we act it,
and back into our shells,
we tortoise folk,
                    so well protected
we can hardly move, playing dead,
                            thus we tell lies
till we do not know what to believe
but brute body can say it better,
gasping out,
                and return to our daily life,
our daily bread.

The night clutches; it is chill,
and I am content with the cold
embrace that touches,
                        this way
I have always loved, why change now,

though I am exploring new paths
at last, to love without loss,

for there is no belonging,
and we all twist and turn,
as the plants writhe
                        into the warm sun,

and we into more than comfort,
into that final forgetting of self,

such a sharp focus, so much
letting go,
            experience of death
before dying,
                as wood burns into flame
and calms down, cooling to ash.

An affair without commitment,
you texted: yes,
    agreed,
I turn into myself to ask
how I could stomach
emotionless sex that seemed
so intimate.
   Your control complete,
all on your terms, much
as you might say you leave it to me
to decide what we do.

     I am sunk down
deep into desire, do not want
the domestic, ordinary days and nights
matched with a belonging, but this
outrageous, separate, sun-spilling
into and out of you,
    so much skin-stimulated
forgetting of all woes.
    But only without
commitment affair, to which,
despite together we have glimpsed
an eternity
   of touch,
playthings of pleasure, I say yes.

Soft and slender as petals,
flesh phantoming out of desire
onto a bed to seek fulfilment
and flow, your limbs
    folding with mine
into felt postures that take us
out of all past, all future,
into a pure now, swept clean

of promises, of caring, cruel
and relentless the honesty
with which we reveal ourselves,
each to each, close up;
                        and then:
cold smile, conventional goodbye,
all turned to trite phrasing
and a letting go at the door,
abruptly shut, right in the face:

all that it was, there is
no meaning as such,
                        only sensation,
and a return to everyday routines,

politeness, the hiding of self.

Not that I ever trusted a word
that you said:
                deceived too
with your limbs and well taken in,
all senses of that, into you, so
it seemed, and fooled by all that thrashing,

not that you cared, we are so far,
so far from that.
                        I was brought
for a moment alive by a panthering
spasm that fell from your lips
as you shrank
                and it seemed
a sharing of self,
                        an opening out,
naked and bare, some game
that you play,

                    which others
do better than me
                        and so I must smile,
pretend I am not bleeding

from so many wounds,
nor wearied by explanations
of how we came to be on this planet.

Just another body,
                        all said and done,
we spoke little, but it was more
what we did that echoes still
through my sense of touching, of holding
tight, of deeper down, into and over
until we might be one, or, for a moment,
think that illusion more real than any,
though all illusions dissolve,
and your body and all
                        its immeasurable,
deep pleasures fading as ever into
lost patterns of possession,
                        falling away,
unless moments will matter
in endless eternity
                        where we are all bound,
and if so I need to be holding you tight.

But our limbs clothed silence
and nothingness was enclosed
                        in the way
you folded inward or out and I was

taking you, home, perhaps, or, simply,

taking,
      as to peel fruit and eat
and feel the supple, sensuous, unlasting
taste of another soul - that spurned me -

but still I am held
                in a suspense
of your singing nerves that seemed
for that time to be ripe song and real
in all
      resonance of your mellifluous moans,
my manipulation
            though subject to yours.

What is the final consummation,
of what, with whom, perfect, complete,
what does it mean?
          It is a long
linguistic derivation, Old French, Latin,
how much further back -
            for a simple agony
of not being -
        let me scream out
how much I have wanted
            you, it was always you,
for to be so alone is the ultimate torment:
I must escape
      but you is
always slipping out of my grasp,
              my gasp.

Not recent, this sense
of the alteration of being
        into a vacuum

of betrayal and absence -
yes, you all melted away, your smiles
fainter -
                I expect it hurt you as well,
but how could I know that
through such distance, of time, of place,
till the illuminated hillside told me
that all was lost, I was alone
but still alive
                and had to endure
forever this bright and immaculate
                                        pain.

And I have endured,
but how much longer
I do not know -
                no point:
I have squeezed enough verses
out of my sores, they are settled now
on the printed page, and can speak,
in faint echoes, of me and my days,
how I never gave up,
                        until now -
would it matter to let me fall
till I won't wake up;
                        I will do it soon
and you shall not see
how far out of sense
I have trodden a tightrope
                        of reason,
taut over chasms I had to cross.

I would rather fall
                than get to the other side
and your hollow applause.

Dying is glorious release, I rehearse
it often, and mix it up
with twining our limbs, breath hard,
we breathe as one - no, as two, as two
always, it is a verse-maker's
sleight of hand to make one of two,
we are always separate.
       It is that
made the man on the other side
of the bridge-rail
     jump.

I could have said, you or me, mate,
it is all the same, we will slacken, each,
into a lump of dead flesh -

leave me alone he screamed,
and stopped traffic:
       drivers
were dead irritated by the delay.

Camus catapulted into a tree,
all the stuff in his head knocked out
by the blow;
    Sartre
carried on preaching until he was old
and feeble - smoking
a part of his debility;
      he had worked up
a philosophy on how to give up,
which I tried, but it didn't help;

later I would succeed and think
how much better to have smashed
into that tree with my head and out

than rambling on with phrases,
oh these endless phrases
      of how much lost,
how much abandoned
     and what the fuck.

Deep-rooted, dormant, subterranean:
is this desire I am talking about, no -

leaves curled up so tight
in their enfolding a flower
will cup out,
    blister light
with frail colour, thrust up, firm
and break surface coming through
as if belonging,
     harbingers of spring,
bulbs, from dark, deep, to smile:

but really I mean persistent-impossible-

desperate-crescent-with-longing-
      desire.

Versifier is a kind and generous
appellation -
    one with Gilbert, Longfellow,
Barham. I am content to let that stand:
I have played with words and put
them in order, assonanced intricately,
with various line-lengths; made
new stanzas, re-tried old ones,

and generally mucked about

with experiments:
             form, rhyme,
half-rhyme, intermittent
couplings - words, I mean,
nothing more.
             Traditional too,
but now I am loose, pirate
of all I felt, as ever, but sure
this time that I have had no home
and will heed no calling back,
but forward,
             inexorable, relentless,
breathless, unsparing, the last lap.

Yet one more exploration of another
body:
             exhaustion sets in. You said:
novelty, nothing important. Perhaps not,
if you are trying to make ordinary
the special bursting of one fruit
and its seeding,
             but that's not how
happens for us promiscuous
enjoyers of glorious outspurting
ejaculation, now and forever;

you added: *means nothing.*
             Anyone
will do, and the title of this book
is belied each time we are
not fussy about what, whom, when,
how and why -
             just like an inquest
we avoid the real questions,
slide shyly yet again

into bed, are not satisfied,
but make do.
         It is hardly heaven.

I imagine the Cretacious-Paleogene
extinction, when most of us mostly
wiped out:
        Jove's thunderbolt
blew the big lizards away, it was
all change and suddenly so, this accident
accelerating evolution;
           we took then
so many steps forward to where we are
now; for, small, feeding our young
from our own bodies,
          hiding away
from all the enormous mouths
that would swallow us whole,
we bided our time,
        kept tight,
dug deep, until the explosion came:
            most
of the predators gone, we grew
into our own,
       started to eat
each other; and with so little
to do in the womb-passages
of our dark tunnels other than fuck,

which is still our primary, blind, hopeless
predation,
      more urgent, almost,
than hunger.

Sniff up, smell is surest,
what stirs in the distance -
to kill or to make your own,
what is the difference?
                    I hear
that bears will smell out prey,
a faint whiff that means food,
so many miles away,
                    and dogs
have a range of smell
we know nothing about, cats too,
all these animals are on the scent -
for something...
                    just like us, we hunt,
all our senses pricked, but it is smell
which floods caverns of longing
and leads us
                    to the end of desire,
the knowledge of self as part
of another,
          whole, yet alone.

How could you know that through
the internet I can source websites
to re-embody you; all your
perturbative postures
                    don't bring
you back, not in a sweet body
to hold or in memory...
                    ...so, have you gone,
when I raise these ghosts
of your pleasure, and please them, each,
smiling or groaning:
                    I develop negatives
of your miscreance, though that means

nothing today, with immediate, instant,
digital satisfaction:
                      you, in your
element and I...wondering
what all this fuss is about - yes, nice
to stimulate and be stimulated,
and I am considerate and kind,
but
    is this weeping or bleeding
of need, mask as you will, a blending
of selves, even if, not love,
something
                real, or a screen image,
flickering, fireworks
                    play with
the sky, dead, gone.

Sex is a lonely experience; odd,
you don't do it alone, not
for the best effects,
                  but it is rarely sharing,
more often confirming
                  our isolation,
distance from others -
                each time seems
more lonely, much as we sigh, moan,
lift limbs -
            all fake; yet not fake,
for this simulacrum of how much
not being alone is a way
we elaborate of not being alone,

as we look deep into others
to find them out as we find ourselves
in a stray encounter, for a time

on a strange island, that could be home,
but once again driven forward
to return, safe
                    in the mirage,
but one day we shall merge into nothing.

Evanescent, fluttering, you all
flitter by, rough Shelleys in a trap
woven from undesire, repeated,
the same throes,
                    but no release,
your need sharp as the tail stings,
mechanical pattern that wounds
as it promises healing,
                    and is always open,
sore, cut, frenzy to drown out
but then, the same disappointment,
once more the long search
for water, dry throat-thirst, love-longing
masked,
                    bandaged in mock brutality,
that hides unbearable hurts:

so that each time you let go
of a lost self you are plunged further
down deeply into how alone
this is all turning out,

                    each time
and forever.

So, bite harder, to show
that it cannot be,
                    the isolation,

for sense rings, we shall all waken,
the dead rise and out of our graves
pyjama-clad or naked move
to a consummation never was ours alive
but holy and healing we shall spurt
out joy, blessing the plants
and find contentment
                              amongst flowers
that do not hide their promiscuous
purpose to set seed
                              and die,
so that something should come alive.

And in the rain as we pulled
between platforms Accrington was erased;
from a train the perspective
is pre-all-painters;
                              the sight
of the streets spreading out like a fan
as it opens to hide, shuts up to disclose-
                              how we can
read a place that we slide up to
and out of, stopping to let them off,
let them on.

        I cannot guess how this town, now,
that town, then, match.
                        Almost a hundred years,
long memory for a human, but I can
stretch that way, heard things, reach
through more than a century,
felt time listening to those
I have known: will someone
do that for me?
                        I don't know.

86

So I scribble lines - the same faith,
whatever they meant, as sketched
game on the walls of abandoned caves,
forever running, lost cries echoing still -

did they think then of us
as I think now of them?

Soon I must stop:
                these words:
go back to tight forms - my defence
against...
            all this fuss - I have already
said; maybe I touch you
with these my exuberant phrases?
So what do I mean - wounds? This
a long licking thereof, it is all
tongues, lick or wag.
                    I have done my circles,
come round once more, again
and again;
            we should part -
I have told you a sort of truth;
you have sort of heard.
                    As much to expect
as anyone dares.
                    Maybe moving to climax
echoes that first big bang, much mellowed,
as echoes are, but still a ripple
from and into the emergence of time.

And that without god.
                    We do not need
a creator, redeemer, giver-of-laws -

to interfere
           in the simple pleasure
of food and fuck -
               we grew so far
on this mucky planet without
the punishment gods inflict, until
they aided enslavers, and then
we were really
               fucked - and most of us
slipped right down, into the mud,
slithered about, groped, felt:
               how much
they gloat, that tell us how to behave.

I like to lay back and let the fingers
explore...
           if it comes to a fight,
will resist, see it
           through
right unto death, not into heaven,
but just seeing it clear,
               seeing it right.

Someone shimmied
               right out
of my grasp, ran on, sidestepped
all I was seeking to question:

brought down limbs
which I could forage, taste
the substance of other, hold,
be tight,
           we could come
to an understanding
               of why so far

out and past you are moving away,
and I did not capture
                              your breath
in my arms; you slid out,
as always, snaking apart,
upfield, far from my touch,
slowly I opened my hand,
                              how much
you did not want
                    to let me, both letting go.

Poem or electric spasm
                    (I do not mean sex)
Stromschlag, or -störung, clonic
tonic seizure, convulsing into a cup
of words, or bleeding mouth,
head, hands -
                    how could I hold you safe?

I tried but ever and always
out of orbit you spun, smashed
into walls, doors, pavements,
                              kissed
concrete, cheeks, palms, scuffed
with dirt and with blood.
                              Yet you soon
knit together, scars faded, you healed quickly
until that last time:
                              fell flat,
no motion, no clawing the emptiness
you felt all around, recuperating, silently,
soberly,
          out of my reach, into
your own interminable solitude.

And through the dark night pounded
the steeds, Erlkönig, or coach to a haven
in past times, fleeing, from fallen-into-
a-basket-heads,
                    wherever
the desolate, mad, death-desperate,
so lonely
                they have to kill
all that smiles,
                    that loves -

and so bereft of all meaning
but to destroy
                whenever it shoots up,
which they have to shoot down.

Paris, city of which to dream the human,
holy, alive, urbane, inviolate,
                so far from those comic
desperadoes, who yet kill, hurt, deny
all that it is to live, as they long
for death, soaked in blood, so perfect
in all that they hate of this our diverse, mutable,
enduring, vulnerable, glorious world -

that they are sick to death
and must kill whatever has life,
and then die
                themselves,

we should pity such poor and helpless
imaginations not even able to smell
a flower, unless they do,
                        and it makes them
retch so that in revenge

                        they pull the trigger
in agonies of aloneness.

What can I do against this devouring-all,
death-entwining hatred of all human
happiness -
            I just scatter
words across pages,
                        they are not bullets,
though sometimes they bite and wound -
not that I have targets...random, too, then?

Maybe. These are unloved and such
is their rage of pain at this not belonging
they have taken as emblem
                a burning hatred
so intense that they feel at one
with an absolute destiny:
                        ironic
in a city where for a brief time
Robespierre ruled, not so different
from them;
                and yet...we must touch them,
somehow, acknowledge their pain
as ours, let them belong, if humankind
is not to be
                so far divided away
from itself that it seeks gods
to put all things right.

But how? How reach such desperate,
lonely people who have no conception
at all of human love and can only
imagine a god who revenges all slights

with a total annihilation.
                    Despair
I can understand, loss, grief, I can build
out of these a sense of my own
unworth
            and the world's unrecompense
for all wrongs -
                    but to kill like this?

I can kill in imagination: often enough,
I'm an animal with instincts -
                        to eat, preserve,
even sex is a sort of predation,
                        perhaps, -
but I wake:
            there is so much to love,
I am often estranged, but to kill...to kill...
to kill - like this? When it comes down to it,
even I
        have never felt that unloved.

It and the sea embraced as the ship
weltered and went down,
                    purists
would say she, but it is my dream:
no panic, no rush to escape -

I was alone and let the decks sink
and I with them, no pain any more,
no sense
            of being left behind
as I was enfolded,
                    but did not drown
and woke on a small raft
                    amongst

wildly heaped waters. I had no control
but was calm and let the waves
heave me
         wherever they would,
for this was where I was going;
and what had been, indelibly, finally
washed far away,
               as if
I had just been born.

How, in my imagination, I have held
you tight, as never to let go,
as afraid to be once more alone,
as to hope
         you would take me
into you, both find peace
from this striving -
          for what?
It's a fake, that we should touch each other,
where what hurts,
         what pleases,
is all one,
        then, into nothing,
dissolve to undo that birth - the dull,
bright pain of a separation -
            were it
folded up into god or human warmth,
how far away and inevitable
seems
      the same repeated frustration.

As light drains away, we are
train-window-mirrored,
           superimposed

or stuck as a transfer on bulked shapes
of an alien landscape
                    streaked
with after taste of the cadent, deciduous
sun, echoing its fall over darknesses' edge.

We speed north.
                    People tap lit screens,
speak intently to empty, voluble spaces,
looking at no-one, talking
                    to thin air,
though their faces follow some conversation.

I keep my phone in my hand to re-read
your short text with a cross:
                    something
has happened: no words of a spell
but hurtling the spread night
dotted with lampglare,
                    it is almost
unbearable, the thought of your breath
on my neck and the nearly-but-not-quite,
slight smile hovering over your lips
and into your eyes -
                    oh, if only
now I could watch your face warm
the sadness I see
                    in your set mouth,
stroking softly your head.

As children, taken aback, we tried
not to laugh at the old man talking
of death.
                    Dad had taken us
to show to the local preacher he knew

from his youth,
                    now dying but ebullient
who told us about the man who died
exclaiming with uplifted arms:

Oh glorious, it is so glorious!
and then hushed and added:
It is all only and ever love.

I have tried to learn that
everything is precious and nothing
matters.
            In the end it comes to the same:

not whom we love, often to distraction,
a way to keep warm, but love itself,
known always by its endless
hiding away,
                its long absence,
our unfed need: until one day
shall we shed all desire,
                        and face to face
see without eyes: is that
                    what the dying man
saw? What he said?

It drains away, the writing-need,
as I feed desire,
                am fulfilled, assuaged,
no longer the endless frustration,
inflicted or undertaken as penance
for all the wrongs of the world, my own
imbalance,
            but simply to fuck
is to fly above all this,

                    how much
the demented show their abstract, ineffable
search for solutions to being alone:

I have found mine: fuck
until you are out of breath, recover,
and fuck some more,
                    it is all we have,
all that made whatever we are
came from a single fuck, an
exploding universe,
                    and it is time
to go, they are making noises
at the bar, clattering glasses - soon
I will leave, have left, no trace, but
my imprint of desire
                    spreading out -
that too is love-preacher
and fucker -
                    we are all one.

I should come to an end.
What
        has it all meant? Who
are you?
        Sleeping peacefully
in a south London grave, or,
on my bed, cuddling, we hold
each other tight...
                    is this real?

I no longer need, I find, but let go
of all, longing, and fall into a simple
peace where I am forever lost
in another - which I have ever done,

and so it begins again?
                        Not
if I can help it! I need release.

Once is enough. Why
                        does it keep
revolving, oh, what the fuck,
ewige Wiederkehr, if that means
fucking forever, I'll go along,

just for the ride,
                        quand même.

Words: to explicate, complain,
reminisce, warn, cajole -
                        oh how it goes on,
once it was fun, but I grow weary,
all but whisper in your ear
that you are special, not that you believe it
but smile,
                whether as giving back, change,
we are all trading, or, in acceptance, a sign
of pleasure.

                I stroke you too and you smile again,
with closed eyes, and look up,
                                expectant as a child:
have I done it again? - warmed up
a ghost into responding, sounding me out,
hollow as echo,
                        reverberating words,
words, settling into speech, meant,
immeasurable,
                        soon swept away
by hunger-tides or washed

97

                        into the arid,
abject waste of a deserted bay:
                            yet I wish
I could creep and crawl forwards
my words into your ear,
                        to your taking in
tenderness, giving it back, till we, both,
satisfied, wordless, full without words are.

It is coming, the time this dissolves,
in cloudbursts of dust, when even that
burns itself out,
                    no clocks - how see
the only good I imagine then?
Well, fields climbing,
                        falling away, trees,
the turbulent, tranquil rivering,
as of desire, rippling through banks -

is that bodies, an open, honest, direct
acknowledgement
                    of how we could close,
seem to be one, a search for godhead
in limbs:
            condemned, no doubt,
by every rule for complete subjugation -

except
        this is a different surrender,
that of the rising sun
                        stroking the cold
fields with a promise of heat.

A song swoops above, crude

and promiscuous, dives, takes me up,
as a bird of prey would lift warm-blood
mammal to eat -
                    gentle in claws,
until a tight squeezing of breath out, relief,
perhaps, except there is no-one to feel
the immense, inert, hollow
                            comfort
of dead.
            Flesh it will eat, the bird,
the song, and I so much deplete
as the exaggerated, invented strains
of amplified melody
                        drown out
the daily dullness all must endure
till the claws of brightness
obliterate and we are one flesh.

Lights on a hillside or far streets
suggest dwellings;
                    I have always warmed
to them, houses or lamps, it is habitation,
lost home, people, the things we do, cook or kiss,
mundane, ordinary or adulterous, discreet,
we are, none of us,
                        perfect; not
steadfast, nor promiscuous as gods, but
wayward at times, at times loyal:
above all we should learn to forgive.

Ambiguous bipeds, we are inveterate
killers of all - to eat or that gets in the way;
food for all appetites, suck, devour, lick up,
we are taking it in -
                        there is more to this

when it comes to memory-mingled-desire:
eat, yes, sink in your teeth, but stand
back, teeth will tear flesh,
                        then, seeing
you separate, letting that be, much
I shall not possess,
                        much shall not grasp,
much shall let go.

Like a familiar tune through my head
you run, a rhythm I can't forget,
to nowhere, returning upon itself
to restate its melody,
                        flattened out
and fleeting the shared moment;
                                the words
too I repeatedly hear, now worn to a shred
of meaning, just there for the sound,
biting away at the way your face so full,

I could not tell whether pleasure or pain,
maybe the concentration on now
comes to the same:
                        so sharp,
what cut into us then, recurring
when no more there, but the endlessly
rippling shadow of what has been,
and the pointless refrain.

Stets verneint - god or devil -
proud ghost always telling us off,
telling us no:
                        you are powerful,
vehement, intractable, forbidding -

have held me back so long, now
I rebel, at last,
                    into my doom,
no doubt, do your worst, whatever it is -
but it was, was -
                    drear the deserts
I could not cross, steep the mountains
I could not scale, deep the mire
I found myself stuck, floundered, flapping
no wings,
                    no Shelley-vans, trapped
between Arnold and Eliot, he flew higher,
than both, though they weren't exactly
earthbound,
                    but caught in the web
of their time - as all - broke out, at last:
he, too, soaring above, majestic, intolerant,
falling,
                    like Icarus, but proud
to have flown so high, to have sunk so low.

I will draw a line, finish, come
to an end -
                    this trawling
through time sufficient, a flavour
of me, in all tenses - tensions,
I could have said, how stretched,
confused, searching semper:
it is all one:
                    we are over, mate,
sliding into oblivion, should cry out,
scream or sing, say stop!
                    It is
never enough, but the sound dwindles,
night supervenes, silence

eventually becomes us all,
empty as space, as space, infinite:
if not rhyme, pattern, which it is,
the same in difference and thereby,
maybe, who knows, who cares,
that we shall come to an end
in rhyme,
        vast, brilliant, indestructible
as all that pulsating
             about and beyond
universe of nothing.

Kiss, Ariel or Caliban, the joke is:
they were one and the same,
           but I did not know
how the long frustration would
wear me down
        till of all affection
scrubbed out, I was desire only, abstract,
indolent, fearing to touch:
        what I needed
was to let go of the needing and float free,

and everything fell into place,
          not quite at once,
it still hurt, but I could stomach that,

at last feeling that we are all such,
and from time to time, fumbling, infamous,
as if gone,
        then found, for a while, in dark streets,
drawn curtains, need pouring out; it happens,
moments of belonging, sense
          that it will be all right,
on the night, as we settle down.

Clandestine, hidden, secret, so little
open,
   kept and enjoyed dark, yet how
you blossom without light, flare
into empty, obtuse silence your obscure,
inveterate needs:
        I, too, take you as mine,
for a time we belong to each other, seem
to meet;
    then you are gone;
the memory lingers...as smell, taste,
faint sound echoing, rhythm,
rhyme - it is all that we have,
        it is all that I want.
Waking, I think you into my limbs;
sleeping,
    I ripple in to your warmth,
soften, sudden, we are almost one -
it will have to do.
      But this is a different
flower from petals of spring !

Oh, but as always I talk to no-one alive,
you or him, all these bodies are dead
that I pick with my vulture-greed, devour,
consume - I was never *auf schweren
Morgenwolken mit sanftem Fittich ruhend* ,
but,
   Icarus-bright, plunged to a meeting
with all that brilliant, extinguishing
sun:
   as everyone here must one day do,
exploding into forever, mortal, doomed,
desperate, mayfly-lit, searching, seeking, for fun.

Unknown, unattainable, how you excite
my febrile imagination in your concentration
on potting balls,
                    bent over the table:
desire, rampant, out of reach, swerving,
till you stretch and curve, are fluent
as time,
            mollient as moments to embrace.

How god must have wondered at his creation,
to fall infatuated into wanting his own
yet other all that was moving;
                        or did he forbid intercourse
with the living and tell us to lie with the dead
where he slept himself,
                        yet watchful to see
there was no resuming of all
that makes us alive:
                    we must choose.
We are neither god's nor gods. We are human,
and must not give up our greatest
discovery:
                invention perhaps,
who knows? We can kill, can destroy,
but are also able
                to build, to write,
to care, and to love.

Wayward, careless of me, negligent,
what,
        is this not pleasure?
You are all playing away from home,
cheating someone you say you love -
and this my revenge
                    for all I must bear

when abandoned, that I have no other now
and drop into dark rivers of dreaming
how much
        I am still alone, but do not
sink; rise, shake my head, swim on:

not to the other side, but to falls
where I gloriously subside, forget you,
come clean, far from drowning,
                surface,
at last, finally breathe.

If asked for an image to round it all off -
I once learnt to scythe.
                Mowing long grass
that way, moving as one from shaft
down to blade -
          that was rhythm:
since, I have only been able to find
that pattern in sorting, in sifting, words:

this now seems done, I am yearning, yes,
as ever, but time seems ripe -
                I shall scythe
as my father fished, the elbow, it seems,
the secret , but motion, curve, flowing down
and out,
        I walk forward, the scythe in my hands,
we are one, cut through:
             this could be sex
I am talking about, or verses, both coming alive -

you could say that, for I care about both,
well worth pursuing though rarely if ever
caught right;

                    no matter, it was not that
I meant, or not only that, but a field
of grass I once mowed with a scythe,
and the people around knew
I was simply doing a good job,
not questioning
                    how my arm swung,
how I tilted the blade.

Time, too, has a scythe,
cutting us down - grim and relentless,
it comes to us all,
                    trip, stumble, we become
feeble and fade out.
                    BUT, would you live
everlastingly, cold as a statue, dead
as an old star, immortal, eternal, frozen
forever?
                    No! Not me! I will burn
brightly in time, consumed, flaming put out,
for the rhythm of blade guides what I am,
fully alive at last
                    and aware of the way
I float through the air, swirl, swing,
curl,
          and cut like a scythe.

It is time! To let go, float out, arms folded
across my chest, fire plays with my limbs,
an echoing, there, of what was;
                    I lie still,
cold as stone effigies supine in church -
did they think they would live forever
and pay through the nose

                     to have monks
sing for their souls, masons to sculpt their
enlivening forms to match when they rose?

I hope they were well rewarded
with heavenly bliss.
                     Good luck!
Earth-bound, fixated on all
that bodies deliver of love
                     expressed
in the here and now, I take my chance,
try to engage
              and slip as we close -

it is potent, falling away and then
thrusting deep.
                I doubt if we do it
dead, or bother with all this fuss.

ANHANG - EINTRÄGE

SWOLLEN UNDERGROUND NUTRIENT STORAGE ORGANS

3.12.14 Decided to visit G's grave. Goodge Street to Tooting Broadway. Cemetery after 3. Eventually found it. Upset. Talked.

28.2.15 G's birthday, our anniversary. To the grave, talk some more.

21.1.15 Imagined that this is what G is saying. Still puzzling why on my birthday, trying to work out what was going on that evening.

28.2.71/28.2.15 G reviews the course of our relationship. It doesn't hurt G anymore, of course, but still seems to hurt me.

8.1.14 Set off 5.45, Bradford 7.45. Busy day in terms of appointments. Soon passed. Left at 4, journey ok, home 5.45.

22.7.15 Pub, joyless drinking again, spending money I don't have.

22.6. 15 Daily Mail: "The E U is celebrating this week. It is 30 years since Europe's leaders signed the Schengen agreement, which threw open internal borders, so EU citizens can come and go as they please.

"There is no better symbol of the EU ambition to banish the old world of competing nation states, each with their own laws, borders and currency.

"'The Schengen Area,' the European Commission's website proudly declares, 'is one of the greatest achievements of the EU.'

"History has a habit of punishing Utopian idealism. For even as the EU celebrates its supposed achievement, the human tide of migrants across the Mediterranean has exposed the historic fault lines at the heart of the European project."

22.3.15 The grave disturbed - bulbs I planted in autumn gone. Do my best to rectify the damage, but have no tools. Whatever foraged didn't dig down to the poems. Hoped for bright petals on G's birthday but the grave barren, neglected but for some leaves from the first plantings.

9.8.09 Empty, hopeless. Silverdale. Tearful. Bought fags, sat with one in the graveyard but didn't smoke it. Total despair.

17.6.66 National holiday in the Bundesrepublik, commemorates the East Berlin strike 16.6.53. As Germans we drive down to Alsace, no passports required, through Strasbourg, and drink wine in Riquewihr.

3.9.15 The pub - he is pressing his attentions; she playing hard to get. A world of their own, oblivious of all else. Must stop staring or they will break out of their cocoon of infatuation and stare back at me.

23.11.54 If I survive this I shall survive anything. But such is the sense of pain and loss, I do not want to survive.

20.8.568 Singapore quayside, seeing off an English minister, and family. Singhalese wife, they are shunned by former friends and colleagues. This the quay we left for England in 1952, without Dad. Conflated in dreams with Liverpool; the ship, the last I sailed on, MS Willem Ruys.

11.9.56 Despite Suez Michael and I fly back today. Roof of Paya Lebar airport , I point out our Air India Super Constellation . Mother bursts into tears. A Chinese woman, total stranger, sitting at next table, cries in sympathy. We board in due course and Michael keeps my tears at bay with funny voices, though I am past tears or laughter and feel dead.

19.2.86 To Silverdale - long time on the lane. We have tea, prawn sandwich, but Mother can barely eat. She says she is grateful - strange smile, or was it? The woman in the cafe says she looks very weak.

10.4.15 How much longer this gnawing pain of remembrance?

17.8.58 White Russian, desperate. Later Dad took me to see F and S. I was trying to persuade him to let me stay, certainly didn't want to go back. Why was his response to bring me here?

13.2.55 Recall nothing of the sermon but remember the Old Testament lesson - 2 Kings 5, Elisha cures Naaman of leprosy, what does it mean?

6.6.15 Felt sick in the bookshop - the endless clamour, a supermarket of commodities to be consumed, every item for sale praised as the best.

22.8.15 Eleven people died in the Shoreham Airshow crash when a vintage Hawker Hunter plane plummeted to the ground hitting vehicles travelling on the A27.

14.11.85 Her memory of recent events dims, but she smiles when she speaks of her childhood and in particular recalls eating black pudding in Accrington market as a little girl not long after the first world war.

17.5.15 Met the owner of the pub jogging on the lanes near the canal.

8.9.54 Liverpool for school clothes, New Brighton , meant as a treat, totally forlorn experience, just disappear down the Mersey, not real.

15.6. 15 Returning from work, train stuck in Accrington a while. Compared the loyalty and affection in the past to the spurious, mendacious, synthetic posturing of this government.

21.7.15 Afraid of being hurt; the bitter taste of disappointment.

30.3.79 Euston Road, on way back to chambers from St Alban's magistrates court in the morning, sudden, furious sense of rebellion, the strangest, surest assertion of self-survival.

23.11.04 Strange day, 20 fags in a row while chatting, to Regen 2000, had to mend photocopier, in meeting room felt ill, taken to BRI in ambulance, did my best to sleep monitored, not easy, a few strange turns in the night, someone dies, someone spews up.

22.7 15 Drove to Buxton - a long way. Stayed to the end, but didn't enjoy the opera, and anyway couldn't concentrate on it. Came home to me than any form of sexual love is now out of the question.

25.7. 15 They seem to present an exultant nihilism, yet cold, calculating; how much carried away by ecstatic destructiveness and how much motivated by a loathing of all that is human, not least themselves; and how much commercially astute, as bankers believed themselves to be.

26.7. 15 Why not let go? The fear that identity would totally fragment? That one would know oneself incapable of love, constancy, loyalty?

26.3.09 Up 6, canal walk. No answer from S. To the flat. The body on the floor. Police - statement till 12ish. To 'Rose and Crown' to tell them.

24.1.15 Walked to Mile End, Saw where we lived, long since pulled down, then Tower Hamlets Cemetery. A board told us bulbs were: **swollen underground nutrient storage organs**. *A bit early for bulbs.*

19.11. 15: On the train back home from London; people on laptops and mobiles. Quite a curt message, with one kiss, and I wonder if, once again, I have allowed myself to be misled and carried away.

17.11. 15 Everybody still trying to come to terms with the slaughter in Paris. I watch the match.

18.7. 60 Dad insists we visit some old man that belonged to his youth. Apparently he is on his last legs. Dad seems to rate him, can't think why.

21.01.06 The canal - almost marching along the verge. Always something kindles a barely smouldering hope into a semblance of flame. I have loved till I am dried out, a stream forever in drought. Death and renewal, sides of a coin, can't be only one of them. Spring will spread here a surge of wanting up stems, but my ghosts are that only, fading, we see, but do not meet - why then hope flickering up in such certain defeat.

15.2.53 Break off some stems of pussy willow to take home to mother. I notice tears in her eyes, but she smiles and puts them in a vase.

14.8.57 Dad takes me to Gawthwaite but then forgets me as he fishes. Bored, I wander off and start to wank - someone shouts at me from amongst the stone rubble, - god, presumably, in the figure of a farmer?

113

114